TO: Wendell Murray

<u>God</u> Bless you!

Sincerely,

Ralph Huling

12/13/10

BIBLICAL AND CULTURAL CONCEPTS OF MARRIAGE AND FAMILY LIFE

REV. DR. RALPH W. HULING

Copyright © 2010 Rev. Dr. Ralph W. Huling

All rights reserved. No part of this book may be used or reproduced by any means, graphic, electronic, or mechanical, including photocopying, recording, taping or by any information storage retrieval system without the written permission of the publisher except in the case of brief quotations embodied in critical articles and reviews.

WestBow Press books may be ordered through booksellers or by contacting:

WestBow Press
A Division of Thomas Nelson
1663 Liberty Drive
Bloomington, IN 47403
www.westbowpress.com
1-(866) 928-1240

Because of the dynamic nature of the Internet, any Web addresses or links contained in this book may have changed since publication and may no longer be valid. The views expressed in this work are solely those of the author and do not necessarily reflect the views of the publisher, and the publisher hereby disclaims any responsibility for them.

ISBN: 978-1-4497-0192-5 (e)
ISBN: 978-1-4497-0193-2 (sc)
ISBN: 978-1-4497-0194-9 (hc)

Library of Congress Control Number: 2010926342

Printed in the United States of America

WestBow Press rev. date: 05/18/2010

This book is dedicated to God, our Lord Jesus Christ, and my family. God has so wonderfully blessed me with an incredible wife who has enhanced my life in every way imaginable, and especially as a Christian. I am also blessed with two saved and wonderful daughters. I am grateful to God for them. I thank God for the privilege to be the pastor of two churches, St. James Missionary Baptist of Columbus, GA and New Hope Baptist Church of Lumpkin, GA.

I consider it a privilege to teach in the National Baptist Congress of Christian Education of the National Baptist Convention, USA, Inc. and in the Georgia Baptist Congress of Christian Education of the General Missionary Baptist Convention of Georgia. I thank God for being saved during my adolescent years at the Greater Beallwood Baptist Church in Columbus, Georgia.

I have two saved sisters, Roeaster and Carolyn, with whom I am blessed to have in my corner always and who have put up with their little brother all these years.

Dorothy Robinson Huling, my wife, Daisha Bianca Huling and Nekita Dovae Huling, my two daughters, I thank God for making us immediate family and I dedicate this book to you for your love to me, support of my ministry, and the work God assigned to my hands. My Mother, who is a member of the church I currently pastor, taught me the love of Christ Jesus by example and precepts and demonstrated the love of Jesus in our family; Mrs. Nettie Huling, I also dedicate this book to you.

Contents

Introduction		ix
Chapter 1	In the Beginning	1
Chapter 2	Defining the Christian Marriage	7
Chapter 3	Marriage 101 for a Christian Woman	13
Chapter 4	Marriage 102 for the Christian Man	21
Chapter 5	Walking in Love	29
Chapter 6	When Trouble Comes	35
Chapter 7	Fortifying Your Marriage	43
Chapter 8	The Proverbs 31 Woman	49
Chapter 9	Enter Children	55
Chapter 10	Raising Your Children Without Raising Your Blood Pressure	61
Chapter 11	The Tie That Binds	69
Chapter 12	Love Never Fails	75
Notes		81

Introduction

The family is the most important institution in society and in the Christian domain. It is the most important because it is the first ordained institution that was created by God at the very inception of time. In this book, we will outline and define the Biblical concepts that insure that the family is maintained and sustained in the manner in which it was originally intended.

In order to fully present this information, it is imperative that we understand the marriage has to be in accordance with God's word before it can be expanded into a solid family base. Husband and wife must be well aware of their roles and commitments to each other, before they can become the strong parents needed to raise children in today's society.

Satan today is making constant attacks on the family; however, his strongest attacks are coming at Christian children and adolescents. His darts can be lethal if the parents are not familiar with his wiles and prepared to battle him with the Word of God as their most powerful weapon. By attacking children, the enemy can cause dissension in a home where parental authority, guidance and discipline has not already been defined.

We seek to present information critical to insuring that the Christian family understands that they are called by God and set apart from the world to reflect the love of Christ by loving each other in a spirit-filled Godly manner. When this is done, truly, ...no weapon formed against them shall prosper.

–Dr. Ralph Walter Huling

CHAPTER 1
In the Beginning

In order to understand the concept of marriage, look at the first couple - Adam and Eve. However, there are critical events outlined in the first two chapters of Genesis that must be viewed prior to delving into their relationship. Note that in the entire first chapter of Genesis, as God created each new thing, He said, "It was good." He was pleased with all he had done in taking a massive void and creating a world.

God then decided that in order for this world to operate in a specific manner, there had to be something or someone on the earth to manage, i.e., rule over the earth. At this point, he created man - Adam. He created Adam to be a ruler and to have earthly dominion over His creation. Note here that God gave Adam a job before he gave him a wife. We will discuss this in depth in a later chapter.

Now, after creating Adam in His own image and according to His own likeness (Genesis 1:26), God reviewed His entire creation with Adam. He gave His command "to be fruitful and multiply" to all of the creatures and birds and every living thing and then declared that it was "very good." (Genesis 1:31).

After resting, contemplating and analyzing His new creation, and giving Adam explicit instructions regarding the Garden of Eden, God actually found something that was "not good." In Genesis 2:18, God acknowledged there was something that was not good - it was not good for man to live alone. At that point, God established the need for man to have companionship.

You must understand what "companionship" means. Adam needed someone to share his day with, someone to communicate with, someone to encourage him - someone to assist him, as defined by God - a help meet - someone comparable to him. God was even aware of the need for a man to pick his own companion. He brought, according to Genesis 2:20,"all cattle and fowl of the air,… beast of the field for Adam to name." Among all of the creatures reviewed, none was found suitable by God and Adam to be a suitable companion. The decision was jointly made by God and Adam, thus indicating that selection of a mate should be a decision that is prayed about and not merely jumped into. Because of the effort that God and Adam put into selection of a mate, every Christian woman should be elated and proud to know that she was expressly created by an omniscient God to be a partner . Imagine if Adam and God had chosen a rhinoceros or a hippopotamus as his mate!!!

God then created a woman and brought her to Adam. It is important that we see that the woman was "custom made" because God knew exactly what would be best for Adam, even if Adam did not know himself. At this point, God had designed His plan, His provision and His permanence for marriage. The woman was designed to complete Adam and to rule equally in oneness with Adam. Note that Genesis 5:1:1 says "Male and female created He them; and called THEIR name Adam, in the day when they were created. They were one in every sense of the word--- all the way down to the name. How much more complete can a relationship be?

Enter the serpent. You know the story of how the serpent came in and deceived Eve and she, in turn encouraged Adam to eat of the forbidden fruit. Adam and Eve were tossed from their Utopian home at Eden and curses were separately placed on the male and the female.

First, the woman, because of her sin, lost her position as equal partner in the relationship. At this point, God deemed that her husband would "…rule over thee…." (Genesis 3:16)., but He also said that despite that, the woman's desire would still be for her husband. This is the beginning of the concept called the woman's "submission" to her husband and one we will discuss in a later chapter on the role of the Christian woman.

Secondly, Eve would bear her children in pain (Genesis 3:16). Until that point, there was no discussion of the man and woman procreating. Also note that the woman was only called Woman (taken out of man). Genesis 3:20 is the point where after God has made it clear that the world will be populated with other people, that Adam names his companion ....."Eve, because she was the mother of all human beings." In this same verse, Eve is the first time that the woman is referred to as Adam's wife. Ironically, it occurs once God has said that children will enter the relationship.

The curse of Adam was the equivalent of a CEO, white collar worker, being demoted to factory worker, blue collar status. Genesis 3:17 let us know that man is now to labor, and labor profusely. He was to understand how it felt to work until the sweat poured from his brow. There would be times when his manual labor would generate only......"thorns and thistles."

With all the odds against them, Adam and Eve were driven out of the Garden of Eden to face a world that they knew nothing about.

CHAPTER 2

Defining the Christian Marriage

Just as Adam and Eve entered into their marriage after being thrown out of the Garden of Eden, disillusioned, confused, and bewildered, so do many Christians enter the state of marriage without a clue of the responsibilities that are required of each other by the Word of God. Marriage is the union of a man and woman, brought together by God and committed to God and their relationship. Anything less than that is not indicative of a Christian marriage.

I discussed man's need for companionship and God's decision to create a special partner uniquely designed for him in Chapter 1. Therefore, apparently, God understood that the male would need someone with him to make him a better man, and God made sure that the helper was "suitable." Just as God created man, He created the male ego. The male ego is designed in such a way that he enjoys having someone to share his accomplishments with - the deal he just closed, the big fish he just caught, the promotion he had been waiting on. In short, the male ego needs a cheerleader consistently on his team rooting for him and encouraging him to be all that he can be. Therefore, marriage is necessary for the companionship God identified that was needed for the male in the Garden of Eden. The sharing that companionship affords to the Christian couple brings them closer not only to each other but to the God who must be the head of their relationship/marriage.

The second factor in an effective marriage is cooperation - Genesis uses the term "help-meet." Cooperation between a married couple is critical and comes only when both parties understand that the cooperation must be mutual. Mutual cooperation breeds a marriage that is fulfilling and complete to both the man and the woman. Mutual cooperation also brings growth into the marriage wherein the couple understands that in order to stay married, they have to understand each other's strengths and weaknesses and work diligently to complement each other in those areas where one or the other needs help.

Opposites indeed attract and those marriages where opposites have attracted are, indeed, very challenging; however, they are not hopeless. In the secular world, the word "compromise" is used to define what is necessary to keep a marriage together when it looks like there is nothing in common or where there are disagreements on major issues. "Compromise" is just that - a secular word. If a marriage is lined up with the word of God, and there is an active prayer life for the couple and understanding of the definition of marriage, that nasty word "compromise" will never enter the home front.

An active prayer life in a marriage is the tie that binds. It leads the couple to the ideal state which is "completion" in the eyes of God. For example, the rib came out of Adam to create a woman in order for that void in Adam's life to be filled. I mentioned in Chapter 1 that God created Woman and then brought her to Adam letting Adam know that this was the missing link that they both had been searching for. It is this principle of completion that lets the Christian know that the marriage is not yours. It is God's and should be conducted in all aspects as God's. By constantly acknowledging through prayer and supplication that God has provided a complete relationship for you, the marriage can only be blessed.

Coinciding with an active prayer life, particularly in times of trouble, marriage has communication with each other as a vital life line. Failure to communicate properly has destroyed more marriages than adultery. Why? Because communication is critical to the establishment of the companionship, cooperation and completeness that God desires for the marriage. In the 3rd Chapter of Genesis, reference is made to God coming to communicate with Adam and

Eve in the cool of the day. God wants to do the same thing today in your marriage!!! He wants to communicate to you openly and without reservation, and He, in turn will lead you both to that place where He wants you to be - abiding in Him so that He can abide in you both.

When the wheels of this three-fold combination of companionship, cooperation and completeness are set in motion, it can only lead to the commitment that God desires most in marriage - complete commitment to Him and complete commitment to each other. Too many times when dissension enters the home, one or both of the partners wants to throw in the towel. Divorce should never be an option as this is not God's desire for the marriage. His Word states, "Wherefore they are no more twain, but one flesh. What therefore God has joined together, let no man put asunder." (Matthew 19:6) and He means just that. He abhors divorce!!!!!!!

Egyptians used papyrus paper. Papyrus paper was made with holes throughout it, but when two piecesof papyrus paper were put together, the holes in the top sheet would cover the holes in the bottom sheet and vice versa. This papyrus paper presents a two-fold concept: One, if the man is the top sheet of papyrus, he provides a covering for his wife - a protector. Secondly, with the two sheets of paper covering each other, there are no holes left uncovered. Each of partners covers the weaknesses of the other. This is God's desire for your marriage - the solid parts of your life cover/match the holes in your partner's life, and together you two can truly become one. That is God's purpose and each partner has his and her own role in ensuring that their marriage meets the standards set forth by a sovereign God.

CHAPTER 3

Marriage 101 for a Christian Woman

The most effective Christian marriage is one in which the husband and wife not only know their respective roles, but understand their roles as they relate to God's Word and to the committed relationship. The Bible says. "Whoso findeth a wife, findeth a good thing, and obtaineth favour of the Lord." (Proverbs 18:22). The key is that if a man has found a wife that knows how to love him God's way, he has found a good thing, but also note that God adds a reward. When the man finds you, he also finds favor with God. The man, then receives a double portion. That should make you very happy, ladies. You are so special, so precious, so wonderful, and so elite that God rewards your husband for finding you.

I told you in Chapter 1 that because of Eve's sin in the Garden of Eden, God said that her husband would rule over her. In short, the man would have authority over her and she would have to submit to him. In Ephesians 5:22, the word "submission" is introduced. A Christian wife should submit to her husband. Now, before the stones begin to fly and eyes begin to roll, let us look at the Biblical connotations of the word "submission."

When the word "submission" for a woman is used, even in Christian circles, it has a lot of connotations for a lot of different people. If you say the word to some, blood pressure shoots up 40 points and they immediately tune you out. They feel that the one saying that she should submit to ANY man is chauvinistic. As Christian women, you must first forget everything you have ever heard or thought about the word "submission" as we delve into God's Word for complete understanding.

First and foremost, please know, ladies, that Satan, the master deceiver, the evil diabolical one, who is at odds with the God of the universe, has done a magnificent job of deceiving God's people regarding what submission truly is. Satan, because he is subversive, pervasive, and seeks to divide God's people, has insured that so many misconceptions and out and out lies have been told about this critical portion of marriage. It is because of the enemy's deception that so much controversy surrounds the idea of a Christian woman submitting to a Christian man.

When the word "submission" is mentioned, the first thing visualized is a 250 pound athletic looking guy strolling down the street with this fragile-looking woman walking ten steps behind him like a little puppy dog following his master. That is not God's idea of submission at all!!!! Therefore, in order to clear your mind of any delusions you may have received about submission, let us first discuss what submission is NOT. I will counteract in this chapter the enemy's lies and place God's truth in its place.

Ephesians 5:22 reads "Wives, submit yourselves unto your own husbands, as unto the Lord." Let us look at this verse, grammatically. There is a comparative word "as". Therefore, then, your submission to God mandates your submission to your husband, but there is grace there! You do not have to submit to anybody else's husband. Remember, you did have some choice when he asked you to marry him. In fact, the word "own" is a Greek word, "idios," from whence we got the English word "idiot." So, you could translate it, "Wives, submit to your "idiot" husbands", but I'll never ever say that. Hmmmm, that in itself can explain some things, ladies.

In all seriousness, though, ladies, submission does NOT indicate inferiority. Eve was cursed in the garden; however, when God sent His Son, Jesus Christ, we were restored to our original state, which for women would mean "equal," however, God does have a specific order for the marriage and the family for very specific reasons. It does not subtract from your equal status, but is necessary according to the Word of God. In the Greek language, the term "submission" is a military term: "gupostophus", meaning to arrange in order/under. A marriage, just as any organization, or even a business, must have some form of order if it is to succeed.

In the beginning, God's creation was done in a very specific order. The Word recognizes that and assigns the order in 1Corinthians 11:3: "But I would have you know that the head of every man is Christ; and the head of the woman is the man; and the head of Christ is God." If God can assign headship to His Son, Jesus Christ, why can He not assign headship to ladies? This is His divine order in the universal government and an order from which we should not stray.

We now have the order, God the Father, Christ Jesus, the man, then the woman. It has nothing to do with superiority or inferiority, because, if we are to believe that Jesus and the Father are one, then God is also recognizing the oneness of the marital relationship while simultaneously placing things in order for eternity just as the doctrine of the Trinity is one of eternity.

Christian sisters, this is submission. Jesus is not less than the Father, but He has chosen to follow the order that was set forth in the Trinity - Father, Son, and Holy Spirit. For you to submit to your husbands is not for you to say that you are inferior to him or that he is superior to you. It simply demonstrates that you recognize God's order. I repeat, in His Word, God has NEVER said that the woman is inferior to the man, or less or unequal to the man. Let's reiterate that with the coming of Christ, women were restored to their original state that Eve lost in the garden. You are NOT unequal. Praise God!

In Chapter 1, I discussed that men and women were both created in God's image. They were then and are now, thanks to the salvation of Jesus Christ, equal in essence in personhood. God is saying that, "I have created men and women both in MY image to portray an aspect of MY being." God hears the prayers of women just as He hears the prayers of men. God forgives the sins of women, just as He forgives the sins of men.

Now, what God has done, in His infinite wisdom, has chosen to place one person in the family to be His primary representative. He has placed the man in a position of responsibility for the spiritual leadership of the marriage. He is to lead, protect and provide. Remember, in the Creation, before He gave Adam a wife, He gave Him a job - to maintain the Garden and be the earth manager; therefore, setting in order one of the first three responsibilities of the man - to be your provider. With the creation of Eve, Adam's job duties were expanded, he was no longer just a gardener and a zookeeper!!!!!! He had someone like himself to take care of, protect and lead. In giving you to your husband, God paid you a tremendous compliment. He qualified you, he highlighted you, he deemed you the epitome of what your husband needed in his life to make him complete.

Submission, then, is not slavery. It is helping your husband, not crawling on your hands and knees at his every beck and call. You are in a critical role as his helper - his assistant. You yield yourself to your husband's abilities so that you can help him and the marriage and the family as it grows. Submission is not subjugation. In the military, the fact that one soldier is a private and another is a colonel does not mean that one man is better than the other. It does not mean that they are not both human beings. It does not mean that one is more intelligent or more capable than the other. It only means that they have different ranks and we know that different ranks/positions involve different jobs.

God mandates that all things be done in "decency and in order." (1Corinthians 14:40). There is a chain of command in every aspect of society and there should be a chain of command in your marriage - the chain set forth by God to make a successful marriage.

I know, now at this point, that there are some ladies really still questioning this concept of "submission." You must know that is a mandate of God set forth in Ephesians 5:22. Your problem with submission may stem from your husband not really submitting to God or assuming his headship responsibilities as dictated by God. Let me assure you that you do not have a problem. Your husband did not tell you to submit. GOD DID!!!!!!!!! If you are not submitting to your husband, you are not submitting to God, and your marriage is, and will always be in trouble and outside of God's order.

By not submitting to your husband, you are disobeying God. As long as the enemy can make you think that this is something between you and your husband and you can make excuses, point fingers, and gossip about it to your girlfriends, the longer you are disobedient to God and the marriage will continue to be in chaos. The issue is between you and the God you say you serve. God is not saying submit to your husband because you love him, because you respect him, because he provides, or even because he deserves it. God is commanding you to commit to that man because you love God and you recognize that God knows what is best for your marriage.

Then there is the argument that your husband is not a Christian. That is even more reason for you to submit. First, God mandated Christians be not unequally yoked with non-believers so the marriage is already out of order and I understand the difficulty in this situation. The Greek word for "unequally yoked" is "heterozugeo" which means an "unequal binding together." We have already determined that God has never said that the male was superior to the female. Yet, even in this situation, where the husband is not a Christian, God gives direction as to how it is to be handled. In 1 Peter 3:1 God shows that He is aware of all things and ready to address all things. He advises women in situations where they have married non-believers, to "be in subjection to your own husbands; that, if any obey not the word, they also may without the word be won by the conversation of the wives..." In this passage, God is saying, "Don't nag. It won't do any good and it could make things worse." Women use approximately 30,000 words per day. Men use approximately 15,000 words per day and listen less when too many words are being spoken. The male ego is fragile and will not respond to nagging, negative talk directed at him or "shoulda, coulda, woulda" from you. This is why, again, God gives specific directions, ladies, to guide you through the submission process.

Subjection is beautiful when done God's way. It brings honor, compliments you, and displays inner beauty and strength - qualities that God desires to see in a woman and qualities that a husband likes to see in his wife. Your words cannot change your husband, but by you adhering to the Word of God for directions concerning your role in your marriage, you can keep yourself in right relationship with

Rev. Dr. Ralph W. Huling

a God that CAN change your husband and keep your marriage in right agreement with the Scripture.

CHAPTER 4

Marriage 102 for the Christian Man

First, ladies, do not be offended that we are naming this chapter "Marriage 102", but named yours 101. Since we learned in chapter three, that the male has a role that comes with more responsibility, we have to dig deeper into God's Word to ensure that your husband understands his role. Did I say that right?

Husbands, it is so very important that you know beyond a shadow of a doubt what God requires of you in the institution of marriage. The essence of the marriage lies in you and your complete surrender to the will of God. Satan will attack you in your role as the head of the household with a viciousness that requires that you be "strong in the Lord and the power of His might…(Ephesians 6:10). You must be able to identify attacks on you and your entire family and ward them off before the union is mutilated or destroyed. Know how to launch your own counter-attack!!!!!

God's plan for you, as the head of the household is based on a two-fold premise - a premise based on LOVE. First, you must love God and acknowledge Him as the head of your life. NOTHING, and I do mean NOTHING - not your car, your job, your golf buddies, the Superbowl get-togethers, your poker games - should come before your love for your Creator. Your love for Him will define your ability to love your wife in the Godly manner required. God loved you so much that He sent His Son, Jesus Christ, as a sacrificial lamb to die for your sins. The happiness and complete satisfaction you have in knowing that you love God and that God loves you unconditionally will formulate the blueprint for your marriage.

The second portion of the two-fold premise is given in Ephesians 5:25: "Husbands, love your wives as Christ loved the Church…." We, as men, have to realize the awesomeness of this passage of Scripture. God loved us so much that He sent His only begotten Son, Jesus Christ, to die for your salvation from sin. Jesus Christ, then set in motion the beginnings of His church. Upon your acknowledging and believing that Jesus died and rose again for you and your salvation, you are a member of His Church and it is for His Church that He was willing to give His life. Therefore, husbands, your love for your wife should match that love that Jesus had for His Church. And you do that, because that is what God commands you to do - not because of any blueprint or plan that you may develop in your own mind or what you and your buddies talk about on the golf course.

I explained "submission" in the previous chapter for the ladies to understand. Many husbands like to blame the wife, saying, "If she'll just submit to me, the marriage will be better." Just telling her that you are the boss is not enough. It may even complicate things. God is telling us that as husbands, the primary responsibility for ensuring that love abounds in the marriage lies with us. If we love our wives as Christ loved the Church, God is telling us that she will respond to that loving stimulus.

Christ never mistreated, abused, humiliated, or in any way deceived His Church. Let us look at ourselves, men. Are we really loving our wives as Christ loved His Church? Are we willing to sacrifice our very life or even our lifestyle for her? If you begin to love her as Christ loved the church, then God will begin to work in her life and reveal to her the things that she needs to work on in her life and in the marriage. God can take a marriage on the rocks and put it back together and create a strong family, but it has to be done God's way. God's way is the only way to have a fulfilling family life.

Loving Christ and loving your wife as Christ loves His Church MUST be the strongest commitments in your life. Christ committed Himself to the Church, loved the Church and acted accordingly. We are not always loveable, men, but Jesus always acts lovingly towards you! His love is unconditional and our love for our wives should also be unconditional - not based on performance - but because God has mandated that we do so in His Word and set the perfect example in Jesus Christ. We are committed to love them, regardless of their actions.

Love is a choice - a factor of one's will, so we must choose to love our wives out of our own volition. We are not talking of that mushy, infatuation, like the way she looks, soap-opera type love. That type of love is not real and will not last. Your love must be the 1st Corinthians 13th chapter type of love that does not envy, that is patient, kind, does not brag, is not proud, rude or selfish, not easily provoked to anger and never fails. This is the real love that God defines in His Word and expects to see in your marriage.

Colossians 3:19 makes a profound statement to husband. "Husbands, love your wives, and be not bitter towards them." "Wow," you say, "She doesn't cook, she won't rub my back when I want her to, she spends all my money on clothes, and she spends all her time gossiping on the phone with her girlfriends who tell her to divorce me." How can I NOT be bitter towards her? You are not bitter because the Word of God tells you not to be bitter. It is not a suggestion but a command.

Many of us learned to be husbands by watching our fathers and many times they became outraged at our mothers and we want to do the same thing Daddy did. With all due respect to your father, the Word of God has given YOU a directive and YOU, in order to keep your marriage in God's order, have to do it God's way. You pledged yourself to be true to her and truth can only come through Jesus Christ. Obedience to God's plan for the marriage will insure that your marriage will remain committed and pleasing in the eyes of God.

God has made you responsible for insuring that every part of the marriage and family align with His Word. He has entrusted you with this and expects nothing less of you but to adhere to it. You are accountable to God for how you handle your marriage and family position. Because you love your wife and are committed to her, you must provide and care for her just as you provide and care for yourself. The Bible teaches us that God will supply all of your needs because He loves you. You, in turn, must demonstrate Godly behavior and provide and meet the needs of your wife.

What is your wife's greatest need in your marriage? She needs YOU!!! She needs meaningful conversation and communication with you. That is the nature of women. While many of you may think that because you bring home the check, pay all the bills, and buy her everything that her heart desires that you have fulfilled your responsibility to your wife's needs. Brothers, women are not like us. They do not think like us and God did not design them to be emotionally like us.

Women translate love by attentiveness and togetherness. Believe it or not, long after you are not the handsome young man you were when you met, and she is no longer the ravishing beauty that stopped you dead in your tracks, women still need to hear the same beautiful terms of endearment that you made when you first met. Women still need the hugs, the kisses, the hand-holding, the special moments that drew her to you from the inception of the relationship - even after the relationship is 30, 40, 50, years old. Your deep relationship with the remote control on the sofa is seen as competition and can place an unspoken divisiveness in your house that you may not even be cognizant of. Husbands, beware, this is when the enemy will come in and attack your wife and drive her to the telephone to listen to her friends ideas on your behavior!!!!!!!!!

When you are the head of your household in the way God has designed, things must change. If you really are loving her in the way that God wants you to, you will give her the attention that she needs. You won't have to worry about her submitting. It will come naturally. You, however, are the key, that will make it that way. God has called and appointed YOU, the male, to be the leader of the family. You MUST do it His way, and according to His direction, for it to work according to His plan. The moment you decide to do it your way, or inject your own ideas into something that God ordained millions of years ago, you have made a terrible mistake and opened a door for the enemy to enter your home.

To be a Christ-like spouse is not to be a tyrant or a dictator. Jesus is a "servant-leader" and that is what He is calling husbands to be - not demanding, but loving men of God with a Christ-like servant attitude. Men, if you resolve today to be committed to your wife and marriage, to act lovingly towards your wife, to care for her at all times and be Christ-like in your leadership, she will respond to you and your love in ways that you would never expect.

CHAPTER 5
Walking in Love

*A*s in any process, it is first important that you first understand what is to be done. We have defined marriage and the respective roles. Everyone understands what is to be done. Now, we look at how we take those roles and put them together so that the couple can learn to walk in a marriage that is pleasing to God.

So far, we understand that the Christian marriage IS a big deal in the eyes of God. It is far more than just a man and woman being together without any sense of direction, purpose, or goals. It is an institution ordained by God that involves sacrificing of self by both a man and a woman and submitting to the will of a God who knows what is best for the both of them.

Genesis 2:24 talks about leaving your father and mother. This has always been difficult for couples. Echoes of the Ten Commandments ("Honor thy Father and thy Mother") resound in the ears of the man and the woman. Many times the couple has entered the marriage financially unprepared, and is depending on Mom and Dad to help out in times of financial hardship. Then, too, many couples feel the need to tell their respective parents - particularly, their mothers, every time there is the slightest disagreement in the marriage. The problem with letting Mom and Dad in on all the details of your marriage is that they will hold against your spouse any negative things you have told them and YOU have created an in-law problem yourself. In-law problems can destroy a marriage. Keep Mom and Dad on both sides out of your marriage. Love them, visit them, develop plans to share holidays with one set or the other on a rotating basis, but you do not need their advice on how to solve an issue in YOUR house.

The second part of Genesis 2:24 deals with "cleaving" to each other. The Hebrew translates as "stuck together". AND YOU ARE. God has given you each other, with a specific plan to carry out and it does not name Mom and Dad as part of the picture. Neither does it name your best buddies or your girlfriends in this mixture. It is your job as a Christian couple to weave a permanent life together - spiritually, emotionally, and physically.

You need each other. Women, remember you were created to be a helper and to complete your husband. The implication, then, is that he is incomplete without you, and therefore, needs you. Husbands, you are to provide leadership for your wife, to protect her and provide for her. She, then, also needs you. The couple is dependent upon each other to walk in the ways of God for achievement of a God blessed marriage.

With understanding of the love God requires, and the need for each other, there must also be trust to solidify the foundation of the relationship. Today is a new day. Even if there were things in the early days of your marriage to breakdown any of the elements, the couple MUST come together in prayer and ask God to place this relationship back in HIS order and believe that He will.

Women want security probably more than men in the marital relationship. The wife needs a husband who has a purpose. If she is called to be a helpmeet, she needs to know how to help her husband. Though communication is necessary, the husband must know how to vent. Sometimes venting can create some insecurities in the wife. Have an outlet, husbands, like the golf course, or the bowling alley, or even the gym when you are frustrated. But remember not to share the particulars of your frustrations with your buddies. Reserve the particulars for God to handle. If men find the need to vent at home, make sure that your words end with, "But it's okay. It's going to be alright." The sense of reassurance you give to your wife is the same assurance that God gives you that if you walk in His ways, He will sustain the relationship.

Husbands need someone who will admire him and hold him in high esteem. They need a cheerleader - someone to boost him up even when all the odds are against him. Men, just as women, want to be appreciated, and even if he does not verbalize that need, he wants to hear that all he does for you and the family is absolutely the best thing this side of heaven! If possible, it might help, ladies, if you visit your husband's workplace to see actually what he does to provide for you.

Husbands want and need someone who will acknowledge his deeds and accomplishments both publicly and privately. It will validate your spouse and make him feel important. Sometimes just reach out and touch your husband's hand and let him know, ladies, that you could not have chosen a better spouse. Husbands, tell your wife how much and how often you thank the Lord for giving her to you. Remember, ladies, he had to find you, but you had a choice in accepting the proposal. His work in finding you was not in vain, and your choice was the right one. That is truly the way God wants the both of you to view each other.

When husband and wife know God's divine plan for their lives, they can walk in true oneness which is the ultimate goal. The minute either of the couple strays from the trail that God has designed, it gives the enemy a chance to come in and work on one or the other.

The natures of men and women were created differently by God for specific reasons, but we cannot stress enough that never in His Word did God say the male was superior to the female or that the female was inferior to the male. What God has said is that they are to walk together in accordance to His Word, adhere to their specific roles in their marriage, and let their Christ-driven marriage impact the lives of our society.

CHAPTER 6

When Trouble Comes

Thus far, we have probably made it seem like everything will be roses if everybody just does what they are supposed to do. As humans, we know that we are going to make mistakes of some sort nearly everyday and that does not exclude in our marriage. What we want to do in this chapter is provide answers to some of the most common problems in today's marriages.

Many couples, because of things that are said on television shows, printed in magazines, or that they heard from their friends or even family members, feel sometimes that they cannot have a good marriage and a fulfilling life. The word "independence" comes up so many times in the media to describe the inner feelings of males and females. We hear that women must be strong and independent and really do not have to have a man in their lives to complete them. On the other hand, we hear that men do not have to be married to be complete - they can live playboy lives and find happiness. This line of thinking is directly opposite from what the Word of God teaches and is indicative of what the enemy wants us to believe as Christians. Sadly enough, so many Christians are succumbing to these deceptions and placing our society and our churches in mass chaos.

The married couple has to have the mindset that they are one as taught in the Holy Bible. They must be committed to God and the marriage to the extent that they hold on to it for dear life. Jesus made an unconditional commitment to us. He sacrificed for us. He looked at a sin-sick world and said, "There is no limit to what I will do for you." This is the way a husband and wife must think of each other when the enemy attacks. They must be aware of what Satan is trying to do and immediately cling to each other to keep from falling victim to the devil's deception.

When the road is rocky, remember that first and foremost, your marriage belongs to God. It is not yours to make out of it what either of you desire. He has given you instructions. Adhere to them! When an army is preparing to engage in battle, there is always a specific battle plan. Each soldier knows what his or her responsibility is in the plan and knows how to execute the plan. The soldier has been taught by trained instructors how to do their respective jobs and what to do when the enemy approaches. Retreating is never an option during wartime. The goal is victory!!! As such, so should be your marriage. God has given you specific instructions based on His infinite wisdom and design for your lives and if followed, the enemy will have a most difficult time engaging you.

Marriage is not easy. It is work. This is why God mandates commitment to the ordinance of marriage. If either of you stop working at the marriage, the marriage will stop working. Marriage is for two people who love God, want to please God, and are willing to serve unconditionally in their respective capacities to reach a common goal of unity.

Marriage is challenging. It is a challenge because love has bound two very different people and personalities together. These two different people will be constantly changing, yet, they must become bound into a permanent relationship. When the storms of life come, the couple has to hold on to this principle of knowing that marriage was a challenge when you walked down that aisle. You must be so rooted and grounded in the Word of God and so determined to please God that you are willing to fight for your marriage. The person that you married seven years ago is not the same person today that they were seven years ago, and they will not be the same seven years from now; however, the God you both serve does not change and His plans for you will not change. Let His Word dictate the direction of your marriage at all times.

Forgiveness in times of trouble is so crucial. You are going to disagree. As a matter of fact, if you both agreed on the same things all the time, one of you would not be necessary! The question is, then, how does a couple agree to disagree? How does disagreement not get out of control? Set forth battle rules. For example, in wrestling and boxing, the referee deems it illegal to hit below the belt. The wrestlers or boxers must shake hands and agree to "keep it clean." So should it be in marriage. God has told us in His Word to "Be angry and sin not." (Ephesians 4:26) There are things that can be said in the course of a minor disagreement, let alone a major disagreement, that can severely wound one or the other of the married couple and cause a tumultuous situation.

Learn how to disagree. Let the disagreement be restricted to the situation at hand. Do not go back and bring into a current disagreement something that happened ten years ago. If one of the partners does that, the other will go back and drag up an event that happened twelve years ago. When this happens, it is obvious that there is hidden anger and/or resentment and neither of the partners has really forgiven the other. Forgiveness means giving your spouse a full pardon, not parole. Parole is saying "I will forgive you if you can prove yourself to me." No, no, no! Marriage means giving your mate a full pardon - unconditional release. And yes, the forgiving process may have to be a repetitive one, particularly for the ladies. Men are more apt to do the same thing over and over again, but in order to keep it all together, you must be skillful in the art of forgiveness. Constantly remind yourself that if you don't forgive your spouse, according to the Word of God, you will not be forgiven for YOUR transgressions.

A married couple must be friends. Their friendship must be both deep and meaningful. We are sometimes more patient with friends that offend us or hurt our feelings than we are with our spouses. We will overlook things our friends say, or consider it as them only trying to help us, but when your spouse says or does the exact same thing, we get upset. Your friendship with your spouse comes first. It is of greater significance than any of your other relationships/friendships. Your friendship should grow to an ever growing love for your spouse.

Concentrate on the feelings you had before you were married. Meditate on the emotions that drew you to your spouse. They are not dead!!! If they were, you would not still be with your spouse. What drew you to your spouse? Sit down together and make a list of things that drew the both of you together. It will surprise and even bring some humor into your marriage. Bear your soul on your list. There may be some things that you adored about your spouse at the beginning of the relationship that you have never shared with him or her. TELL IT NOW!!!

If there is a storm on the horizon, listen to your partner. He or she may be looking at things from a totally different perspective than you are. The biggest problem that women have with their spouses is that they do not listen. Men need to learn how to acknowledge your wife's words. Just saying "uh-uh" is not enough. You must hear what she is saying and respond in an appropriate manner. When she asks "What would you like for dinner?", she is saying, "Honey, I want to please you." Or, "Honey, I have run out of ideas for dinner, what do you suggest?" Your response of "Whatever you cook is fine." immediately places a gap in the communications process. She shuts down and feels unneeded and unappreciated.

By nature, men are more compartmentalized in their conversation; however, in a strong marriage, the husband must make every effort to expand their level of conversation and talk to their wives - even when the Super Bowl is on. Then, too, wives, you must understand that men talk less than women and do not nag them about their seemingly lack of compassion or interest in what you have to say. Again, when you communicate effectively with each other, problems like this can be resolved.

Finally, when you feel like your marriage is headed for trouble, both parties have to shift their focus - QUICKLY. One of you must begin to focus on the positive, rather than the negative aspects of the situation, take hold of the ship and steer it back into safe waters. Don't allow your marriage to get in a rut. That is a trick of the enemy to make you start looking outside of your marriage to find other ways to combat boredom. By shifting your focus, you are acknowledging that all marriages have problems, but if you stay focused on the problems, negativity will become a permanent resident in your home.

The easiest way to fight any problem, any turmoil, or any dart that Satan throws into your marriage is to realize that neither of you is perfect. Know that only in Hollywood is marriage a forever beautiful, forever awesomely sex-filled, or forever "rockets red glare, bombs bursting in air." The Christian couple has to know the difference between fantasy and reality and act accordingly. When it seems that boredom is at its worse, this may be the time for the couple to stop and do something fun together. If finance is a problem, a simple long relaxing drive in the country can do wonders. It will free your mind just for a little while to focus on each other, rather than the problem. That is your ultimate goal - to focus on each other when it looks like there is nothing else to do. Let your God keep you in tune with each other. He knows all the right notes, can make the melodies right, and compose a symphony of your marriage that is matchless.

CHAPTER 7

Fortifying Your Marriage

We have defined the roles of husband and wife in a Christian marriage and let you know that all will not be perfect even if you adhere to your roles. We, however, did not dig deep into the process of actually being married and fortifying and solidifying the marriage. We mentioned that it is hard. We said that it is hard work. We acknowledged that problems are going to arise. All of these set the foundation for a good marriage. They are just the beginning.

In the Bible, the word "know" is used to indicate "intimacy." In English, when we "know" someone, we are aware of whom they are, their likes and dislikes, their wants and their needs, and their desires. Both definitions are vital keys to a successful marriage - knowing your spouse and a meaningful intimate sexual relationship.

If you want to have a successful marriage, there are three factors that enable a partner to "know" their partner. Each of these factors are Biblically based and help to meet the needs that each member of the marriage has. First, Ephesians 5:18 says, "Be filled with the spirit…" You can never be the mate you need to be without the Holy Spirit. The Holy Spirit empowers you to be the person that God would have you to be. The Holy Spirit gives you the boldness and authority to rebuke Satan when he attempts to get you or your marriage off the path God has formulated for you. The Holy Spirit leads you to all truth, about your God, yourself and your spouse. God, then, has equipped you with a helper, to assist you in your marriage. Call on the Holy Spirit to lead and guide you!

Secondly, the married couple must rely on their faith, confidence and trust in the God who knows them better than they know themselves. The divorce rate in this country is higher than 50%; however, in Christian marriages where couples regularly pray together, only 1 in 10,000 marriages end in divorce. Astounding! Christian couples must rely on their faith in God and His Word for building and maintaining their marriage. Jesus said it best in Matthew 7:24 -26… "…the house built on the rock stood, while the house built on sand collapsed." When you pray together and lean on Jesus and each other, you will really fortify your marriage. If you don't, you will find yourself leaning on material things or leaning on yourself. That is tantamount to building on sand! In my role as a Pastor, men often come to my study to talk to me and confide in me the fact that that their marriage is breaking up. Their rhetoric is always the same. They do not understand why their wives want to leave. These men have given their wives everything - exotic vacations, expensive jewelry, beautiful houses, luxury cars, and yet their wives still want to leave. What these men have failed to realize is that they built their relationship on sand - material things - things that will not last. They never built on the rock of Jesus Christ.

When driving down an interstate highway, there are many exits. There are exits showing what is available at each exit - hotels, malls, restaurants, gas stations, etc. Your marriage is just like that interstate highway. There are many exits - many opportunities to leave the marriage. If the couple does not have Christ first in their lives, they might pull off on one of these many exits and miss the destination of their journey. Do not throw it all away because of some bad days in your marriage. Sometimes the very thing that annoys you the most about your mate is what really makes them special!!

The third factor in fortifying a marriage is understanding exactly how to meet the needs of the other. Not surprisingly, the basic needs of men and women are different and they react differently when their needs are not met.

Men have five basic needs: sexual fulfillment, recreational companionship, an attractive spouse, domestic support, and admiration. These needs are imperative because of the nature of the male ego. Though the male ego is dominant, it is still quite fragile, if not more fragile, than that of the female. Therefore, the wife has to look at her husband, look at herself and identify the areas where she is falling short and pray for God to guide her - not only in ways to strengthen her in those areas, but to enable her to actually MEET her husband's needs.

Women, too, have basic needs: affection/touching, communication, honesty and openness, financial support and family commitment. If you examine the needs of a woman and then compare them to the needs of the man, you will note that a woman's needs are more intimate in nature than a man's. Women desire affection and romance whereas a man's desire is sexual fulfillment. Women are emotional creatures and their spirits are more easily wounded than men. When the spirit of a woman is wounded, a man can forget any ideas of intimacy until the opportunity presents itself to discuss the situation. She will discuss it later at a time when her spirit is no longer wounded. But, until that time, most men will not even recognize that a problem has arisen or will be extremely perplexed as to his wife's behavior. . A woman's desire is to vocalize her feelings to her mate in order that a quick resolution of the problem can be reached. She understands more than a man the dangers of hidden resentment.

In direct contrast, when a man's spirit is wounded, he may not display any signs of dissatisfaction. Just as he may not recognize his wife's wounded spirit, he many simply brush off his own feelings and carry on as though everything is just fine. His failure to recognize that his wife is upset about something unbeknownst to him, is indicative of the fact that he needs to learn to listen. He needs to not only listen, but also recognize her unspoken body language - those things that let him know that all is not well. A husband has to learn to patiently listen to his wife with his ears and his heart. He has to recognize that something is amiss. If not, he will have a wife that cease communicating to him and will feel he does not care or that it does not make a difference what she says. It is safe to say then that if a couple adheres to Ephesians 4:26..... "Do not let the sun go down on your wrath....", then whatever issues they confronted that day, will be resolved and the next day can be a blessed new day.

Satan deals with the subconscious mind intensely during sleep. God is aware of this and therefore warns us in His Word - DO NOT GO TO SLEEP MAD AT EACH OTHER!

The three fortifying factors of marriage can be summarized into seven concepts we have discussed in previous chapters and must be reiterated here:

1. Touch each other often.
2. Spend time with each other.
3. Accept each other unconditionally.
4. Encourage each other with words.
5. Accept each other unconditionally.
6. Be committed to each other.
7. Laugh together often.

I believe that God wants us to enjoy heaven on earth in our marriage. God has said that if you obey his commandments…. "your days will be multiplied, and the days of your children, in the land which the Lord sware unto your fathers to give them, as the days of the heaven upon the earth…" Deuteronomy 11:21. God wants your marriage to be strong and solid and it begins with both parties having an attitude adjustment and being consistently aware of the concepts discussed in this chapter. By setting the marriage as the top priority, only the best can happen in the lives of you and your mate.

CHAPTER 8

The Proverbs 31 Woman

Yes, we have discussed the woman and her role in marriage but this book would not be complete without discussing the phenomenal exemplary women described in Proverbs 31. We are not downplaying you, husbands, but this woman is one to be admired and respected by BOTH married men and women. She represents a woman who knows whom she is in Christ, whom she is to her husband, who she is to her family and who she is to herself. Each and every man should pray and ask God to lead Him in the direction of the nearest Proverbs 31 woman!

The woman described in this passage understands her role as a wife. She is not frivolous with the income of the household and according to verse 10 of this chapter, he trusts her implicitly. He knows that she is not going to waste money on things that are not necessary. She is not going to deviate from the budget that they have together put in place - the budget that will keep the household financially afloat. A woman that understands that the family must be financially sound is a good investment for a man!

She is committed to him and loves him to the point that she will never seek to do him harm. This does not necessarily include physical harm. This means she does not denigrate him to her family and friends. She prays for him and desires the best for him as he leads the household in God's ways. She keeps him covered under the blood of Jesus, knowing that with this covering, the whole household will be blessed.

She is multi-talented. In his passage of Scripture, she is a seamstress. She makes all of the clothes for the household, selects the best cloth ("scarlet" - Proverbs 31:21) knowing that she has the entire house dressed appropriately by the work of her own hands. Now, not all women are seamstresses, but oftentimes, the emphasis is placed on dressing the children better than she dresses her husband and herself. The children wear tennis shoes costing $150.00 and Mom and Dad visit the local discount store for nearly all of their apparel. The couple calls it "sacrificing for the kids." I call it a gross misunderstanding of the concept of family.

Because the husband is the head of the household, the rest of the family is a reflection of who he is and how he looks - the image he conveys. The Proverbs 31 woman is aware of that and insures that the provisions the husband makes for the family for clothes is well-used and allows for the whole family to show how God has blessed them. This woman is proud of her husband and wants him to know that she is proud of him. Verse 23 says "Her husband is known in the gates, when he sitteth among the elders of the land." Her husband is somebody special in the community and she feels she is a part of that respect he has earned because of her contribution to his image.

She is an astute businesswoman! Let me say that another way, the Proverbs woman has a job. Verse 16 says "She considereth a field and buyeth it; with her hands she plants a vineyard." Christian woman, do not be deceived. It is okay for you to work and assist your husband financially if that is his desire. It may be necessary for you to work in economic times such as these. The goal is to do what will best work for the family unit as directed by the husband as he listens to God. The Bible never said a woman was to be a stay at home Mom. The Bible does demonstrate ways to handle the tremendous responsibility of being a working wife and mom. If, however, you are fortunate to stay at home and strictly handle the affairs of your home for your husband, do not look down upon yourself. Do not let your friends make you feel that you are inferior because you do not have a "career." Your home and family is just as important as any job - take pride in the fact that you do not have to hire babysitters and entrust your children to the care of others. Be proud that you can do a myriad of things during the day that working mothers cannot do. Many times you are MORE of an asset to your husband because of your availability.

The Bible says the Proverbs 31 woman rises early. This is her "Jesus time", her prayer time, her time to reflect on what this day will bring. She rises early and also prepares breakfast for her household. It has been said that we are raising a whole generation of young ladies that do not know how to cook unless it is microwaveable! Fast food restaurant profits continue to soar. Children are topping the obesity charts. Nobody is saying that breakfast has to be a five course meal of pancakes, bacon, eggs, hash browns and six kinds of milk. A simple bowl of oatmeal is just as nutritious. The breakfast schedule can rotate. There is nothing wrong with the husband cooking breakfast for the family. However, the quality time of a family eating together at least one meal a day has a tremendous impact for the household.

The Proverbs 31 woman is not only a woman of spiritual and emotional strength, but she also tries to remain as physically fit as possible with her difficult schedule (Verse 17). She understands that when she comes home, if she works, that has to leave her job at the job. Her family needs her and she does not let them down. She comes home ready to listen to her husband and her children as they, as a family, discuss the day's events. Husbands, you, also, must learn, to leave your job at the job. When you enter your home's threshold, enter with a desire to share your love with your family attentively and with concern.

This woman is confident because of her competence. Ladies, this is the way all Christian wives should be. You should know that you are a good wife and mother. Know that you successfully juggle your responsibilities with ease and grace. Pat yourself on the back sometimes. Look in the mirror and thank the Lord for you being the wife and mother that you are. You will be amazed at how this will transform you into a more positive mate in your marriage.

Women by nature are compassionate and the Proverbs 31 woman is no different. She assists her husband in ministry. She has a passion for helping the poor as Christ has commanded. Together, the couple has worked and handled their finances in such a way that they are able to be a blessing to others. They give God His tithes and offerings first, knowing that by doing so, their needs will be provided and other blessings will come.

This woman has developed wisdom through her faith and trust in God and watching God move in the life of her husband. She knows when to speak and when not to speak. When she speaks, she chooses her words wisely so as not to offend. She has a beautiful inner spirit that is easily recognized by her husband and others because she is completely fulfilled and satisfied as a helpmeet and mother. Her husband and children both are proud of her and verbally speak their praises to her. She knows she is loved and that makes her work harder to keep that love and respect.

She is a woman of moral integrity. She does not have time to gossip on the phone with friends about meaningless garbage. The life that her husband has provided for her and the family is a source of pride for her and she does not see the need in wasting family time. She has an active prayer life and prays for her husband, the marriage and their children daily. People recognize that she is "different." They see that the whole family is "different." This woman compliments all that her husband is.

Men, you deserve nothing less than a woman of her caliber. Seek diligently until you find her. Better yet, if you are the man that God has ordained that you be in the marriage, your wife will be a Proverbs 31 woman because she will do all she can to show the world whom YOU are. She will call your name with dignity, respect and pride each and every time. Could you want anything more of your wife?

CHAPTER 9
Enter Children

From the minute of the couple's first infant's cry, the marriage boards a different ship. No, the different roles do not change. The man still remains the head of the household, the woman is still the helpmeet, but now responsibilities for both members of the couple are increased. Note also that God's order adds an additional link: GOD, JESUS, MAN, WOMAN, CHILDREN. For the man, his responsibility now increases from protecting and providing for his wife to now protecting and providing for his wife and children.

When the first child is born, often difficulties arise. The husband feels left out. He may feel that he is not getting the attention that he once got from his wife. He may even experience feelings of jealousy and insecurity and question the degree of his wife's love. "Does she love the baby more than she loves me? The baby certainly is getting more attention than I am." Men, these feelings are shared by most men when children enter the scene.

Believe it or not, husbands, this is the time when your wife needs YOUR attention the most. She actually may be overwhelmed at the level of HER new responsibilities. Now is not the time for the couple to fail to communicate their needs. This is a critical time! That beautiful little bundle of joy that God has brought into your lives is going to take away a lot of the time and attention that you once had for each other.

First, husbands, the Bible does NOT say that it is the woman's responsibility to raise the children. In fact, most Scriptural directives aimed at child-rearing are directed at the father. It is the wife's responsibility to carry out her husband's plan for raising their children based on the Word of God. Again, this does not mean that Mom does not have any input, it simple means that the Word of God is the outline for raising the children in order that differences in parenting styles do not interfere with the marriage.

How does a couple make sure that they still have time for each other - quality time - when children, especially small ones, require so much care? First, share in the responsibilities. It is just not Mom's job to change diapers, Dad! Secondly, find a good Christian babysitter. If the child's maternal or paternal grandparents are nearby, they are the ideal people to baby sit while the two of you enjoy a "date night." Third, be constantly aware of each other's feelings and make sure that one or the other of you is not feeling alienated. Fourth, realize that the baby is an extension of your marriage, not an added burden. Children are sent by God to be a blessing to you - a way for you to leave a legacy of the Christ in you and your marriage. Fifth and most important, put God first in your marriage - NOT JUNIOR!

One of the biggest problems in marriages is that Mom has been taught by her mother that no man should come before her children. This myth has been sent down from generation to generation and one that I believe has fostered so many of society's problems now. Once the child comes, Mom takes over the raising of the child, sets forth the rules, and completely omits Dad in the process. She determines when, where, and how everything is done when it comes the child/children. Dad has no input, is not allowed to have even an opinion, and is only told what's going on if it's a major disciplinary affair. Ladies, when you behave as if these are just YOUR children, you will isolate your husband. After a period of time, he will cease to even attempt to have conversation with you or the children. He will shut down and let you handle it. You will have on your hands manipulative children who will place you and Dad at odds because Dad is not really considered in the picture. You will also breed a husband who may find other ways to meet his basic need for companionship because all of your time and attention is directed at the children.

Men, beware! When you notice that your wife is pulling more away from you and being more Mommy than wife, take immediate action. This is a time for you to initiate DIRECT communication - even at the risk of laying down the remote control! You are the head of the household, the husband and the father. Now is the time for you and your wife to communicate as husband and wife regarding your individual relationships with the children. Each of you should have relationships with the children and the relationships may not be the exact same; however, you all must be on the same sheet of music regarding YOUR relationship as it relates to the children.

The children have to know that Mommy and Daddy both love them and both of them are responsible for their well-being. Believe it or not, children will learn this by seeing for themselves the love you have for each other. Children will learn through the interaction of Mommy and Daddy what their roles in the family should be. There are households where children are in charge because Mommy and Daddy have allowed themselves to lose control because the marriage is out of control. Parents have to be adherers to the Word and raise the children in the fear and admonition of the Lord. They simultaneously must insure that their homes are in order with God's word. Everyone in the house can then know their respective positions and can bind together in a cohesive family unit.

Just as other people need to remain outside of the marriage when problems arise, so should they remain outside when problems with the children arise. Parents have to communicate with each other first, develop a plan of action, and then take the appropriate action necessary for swift resolution of the problem. If your opinions are different, NEVER, EVER, disagree about the children in front of the children. Go into another room, sit down, and calmly discuss the problem. The two of you must always present a united front before the children if the family is to work properly. Your children must know whom is in authority and how to react to the authority figure in a way that is appropriate. How you react to each other as a couple is the greatest example for your children to follow.

Teach your children how to communicate to their parents. Parents, please have a listening ear. Sometimes, you can learn from them. The more you listen to your children, the more you will learn about them and the world that THEY live in. You will be better prepared to counterattack Satan when he comes with his best shots at your children. Recognize the fact that Satan uses your children to enter your home. They are easy prey. They do not have all the tools yet to fight him. Be aware of this at all times. Not only should the couple pray together, but designate a time for family prayer. Teach your children how to pray from the time they can talk. Teach them the reasons for prayer and the power of prayer in their lives. Prepare them for the enemy, but you always have their backs. Always be there to lead and guide them in the ways of the Lord. In order to do that, you MUST communicate with each other, your children, and with each other AND the children.

CHAPTER 10

Raising Your Children Without Raising Your Blood Pressure

We live in a world where parents are having a difficult time raising their children to be resourceful, responsible, and above all, respectful with high levels of self esteem. In this chapter, we will discuss some parenting tactics that will work if adhered to. Being a parent myself, I have been able to draw so much from the Word of God and my own experiences to provide some information that will be useful to Christian families.

First of all, let us recognize where parents learn their parenting techniques. We usually duplicate the parenting skills that were utilized in the homes we grew up in. That could be a positive thing; however, much too often the homes we grew up in were dysfunctional. We, then, pass these dysfunctional skills from one generation to another. Parents model certain behaviors and children mimic those same behaviors as adults. Have you ever heard the phrase, "I open my mouth and my mother comes out?"

I was one of those exasperating children that was difficult to raise and I learned about parenting retrospectively. When I first became a parent, I found myself parenting in the manner as my father. It was not working with my children and I had to come to grips with the fact that I was not my father and my children were not me. I was so busy imitating my father's parenting that I did not even stop to realize that I was raising two daughters and he had raised a son!

I called a "roundtable" meeting and apologized to my daughters for some of the mistakes I had made as a parent and assured them that from that point forward, I would strive to be a better parent. I let them know that I needed their cooperation. We made a covenant to work together and I am proud to say that I now have two wonderful, professional daughters whom I love and respect very much. Thank God for that!

Just as every company, organization, school, and church has rules, couple must have rules that they set in place in for raising their children. If a child is going to learn and comply with the rules of society, he must learn to follow rules at home. If children are not taught to follow rules at home, they will experience difficulty complying to standards set at school, at church, later on their jobs, and ultimately in their own married lives.

Rules must be clearly stated, defined, and fair. Rules must also meet a child's ability to be able to comply with them. For instance, Jamaal, asks his mother, "Why is it that I have to wash dishes every Tuesday and Thursday nights as one of the rules in this house and the rule doesn't include Sidney?" Mother replies, "Because Sidney is three years old!" Jamaal sees something that Mom has missed. Yes, Sidney is only three, but he should begin to have his own set of rules in place. Sidney, at three, is not too young, to perhaps hand Jamaal the dishes as he washes them. Sidney is not too young to help Jamaal wipe off the table. By having both children adhering to a set of rules at the same time leaves no room for claims of unfairness or favoritism to come into the picture.

I remember on one occasion, I came home from work early. My daughters had just begun to ride the bus from home to middle school. I did not understand their elation at their newfound freedom from me taking them to elementary school. They knew to get off the bus, come home, and begin their homework. On this particular day when I got home, one of the neighborhood girls was sitting in our house with my daughters and they were not doing their homework. My daughters' friend was a little older than my girls and I could tell that she was manipulating my daughters. I asked the neighborhood child if her mother knew where she was and she replied that her mother was not at home. Good parents have built-in radars and I sensed that the girl was not telling the truth. I called her house. Her mother, indeed, was at home, and answered the phone. I explained the situation and the child's mother asked me to send the child home.

A week or two passed by and I came home from work early again to find the same scenario at the kitchen table - my daughters and their friend and nobody doing their homework. I was then incensed. I felt like my children were taking advantage of this new parenting approach. After questioning the child again, I determined another hoax was being schemed. After I called the child's parent and she went home, my daughters thought I was really getting ready to put them through the wringer. Then, from out of nowhere, I had this uncontrollable laughter. The harder I laughed, the more confused my children became. They asked what was happening. I informed them that initially I was very upset, but then I realized that I had never made any rules in the house that pertained to them not having anyone as a guest in our home without permission! I then made it a rule that my daughters were to invite no one to our home when their parents were not present without permission. I repeated the role every morning after breakfast to them until one morning I actually forgot. I came back in the house and they simultaneously said, "Daddy, we know the rule!"

Rules for your children set boundaries and act as guidelines just as the Word of God is the guideline for a Christian life. When there are rules and guidelines, behavior changes in your child. Learning is any relative change of behavior brought about through an experience. My mother told me as a child never to touch an iron because it was hot. I was not satisfied, as are many children, until I touched it. It was at that moment that I learned that the iron was indeed hot as my mother had warned me. That experience changed my behavior and I never touched a hot iron again.

It has been said that if a person hears something a nominal amount of times, they will retain it. Family rules must be clearly established and defined. An example of a rule for school: "You will go to school every day, do whatever your teacher tells you to do, and display good behavior at all times." If the child fails to follow this rule, then there will be consequences both at home and at school.

Our children must be taught by specific rules what is required of them.

They must first be taught to obey their parents. This is the first confidence that must be established. Christian children must know that their parents are requiring this because the Word of God requires it. When children are loved in a Godly manner, as we set forth rules that will lead to successful, productive lives, they will respond in an appropriate manner. Children must be taught. Parents, you cannot assume that your children ought to know certain things. It is your job to teach them everything that they need to know about their position in not only your family, but in their church, in their community, and ultimately in God's kingdom! Never give or entrust this part of their education to anyone.

After the rules have been clearly stated and defined, there must be a system of monitoring. Monitoring gauges the level of compliance with the rules. Children are like new recruits in the military. They never do what you expect, they do what you inspect! Children realize that many times parents fly off the handle and make rules out of anger that they do not intend to, or cannot monitor. To a child, when parents follow up and monitor behavior, this is actually a sign of love. Children do not care how much you know, they want to know how much you care. Is not that like what we want from God? We know that we will never understand the extent of His power and greatness, but we find comfort in knowing that He loves us unconditionally.

Once upon a time, the extended family assisted with monitoring the behavior of the children. "Big Mama" helped with the child-rearing and monitoring was not as difficult. Times have changed. Now even "Big Mama" may still be gainfully employed and not able to commit to staying at home with the children. Everyone else on the block is also employed. Latch key children abound - children who come home from school to fend for themselves until Mom and Dad come home from work. Unless rules are set in place and understood by your children, phenomenal problems could arise. However, latch key children can be monitored. Require them to call you at work to check in with you and your spouse. If you have the flexibility, arrange to come home early occasionally. Get to know your neighbors and ask them to let you know if they see anything going on at your house that you would not condone. Give your neighbors your work and cell numbers so that they can contact you immediately.

It is amazing that when people drive through the school zone and there is only a crossing guard standing there, many will disregard the speed limit of a school zone. However, if a policeman is there monitoring the speed limit of the traffic, each and every driver will slow down and regard the policeman's presence. Why? The policeman is able to cause some consequences. So it is with parents, if we just create rules and never monitor/follow-up on them, your child will disregard them. When children realize that parents are going to monitor their behavior to ascertain that rules are being followed, they will be better behaved children.

Children pay close attention to their parents - more than parents realize. They know when you mean business and when you do not. They are able to manipulate parents because they observe them closely. They know what will work on Mom and what will work on Dad. We learned in an earlier chapter that this is why it so important that Mom and Dad are consistent and work together in implementing viable rules for the home. Please believe that our children know us very well! This is also true as it relates to grandparents. Children will have grandparents at odds with parents simply because of their ability to manipulate and because of their ability to study and learn parents.

We have stated that because of economic times, it is most likely that both parents are employed. This can present a challenge to monitoring your child's behavior, but it is not impossible. We mentioned two options above: having your child check in with you at your job and getting to know a neighbor that may be at home and giving them your daytime contact numbers. Your children can also be monitored by involving them in wholesome after-school activities - sports, cheerleading, scouting programs, boys/girls clubs, etc. Talk with your pastor about church activities that can begin immediately after school - youth Bible study, choir rehearsal, or tutoring programs. These are all programs that will assist you in teaching your child rules and also help in building your child's self-esteem, teach him/her how to appropriately interact with others, and develop his God-given gifts and talents.

When it comes to monitoring your child, there are four things that good parents should know at all times:

A. Where your child is.

B. Who your child is with.

C. What they are doing.

D. Whether you approve of the above.

The last part of discipline and rule-setting is that parents should implement "consistency." Both parents and rules must be consistent. Children learn and obey by our level of consistency. This is where the proverbial rubber meets the road. There is an aspect of parenting called "shaping." Shaping comes through successive approximations. In our adult lives, God is our "potter" and He molds and shapes us after His Will. The process of God molding us as parents must trickle down to us shaping our children. For the child to benefit from rules and the monitoring process, consistency must exist. So as the Word of God is consistent and non-changing, so must our directives to our children must be in order that they will grow not only in their earthly ventures, but more importantly, in their spiritual lives.

CHAPTER 11

The Tie That Binds

The family unit is the most important organization in society. Within that unit lies the key to a better church, community, nation and world. How we follow God's design for the marriage and family dictates what will ultimately affect those around us. This trickle down effect, if practiced by all Christian families, could bring about a transformation that could be revolutionary!

When a family falls, destruction of some sort strikes each member of the family, particularly the children. Husband and wife may be lashing out at each other with viciousness while the children sit back and may be stuck in the middle. The children may be used as tools in the downfall of a marriage -submitting their young minds to manipulation and deception. Children suffer severely when a family splits. They may be forced to choose between Mom and Dad. Mom and Dad put pressure on the children to declare their allegiance to one or the other parent. What a horrible responsibility to put on a child who has nothing to do with the problems the couple is having!

If you do not wish for your family to be a statistic, be mindful that there is a force that has risen against the family and God has already given the family a strategy - but it is a strategy that requires recognizing that there is a problem. 2 Corinthians 10:3 says, "For though we walk in the flesh, we do not war after the flesh." You are not battling with a human instrument. You are in warfare with Satan and as he brings anger, resentment, confusion, and animosity into your household, you must recognize it. You must know and learn to use a weapon that will be effective in countering all the problems the enemy brings. That weapon is the Word of God. In His Word, God advises, counsels, and leads your family in an effective counterattack.

The head of the household, the husband, HAS to understand that it is the desire of Satan to bring each member of your family down to his feet in order to crush them. It is your responsibility to constantly be on the look-out - a sentry - for strikes. You must be constantly aware of your role to lead and protect your family. YOU must set the example by leading your family according to John 4: 23-24: "worship Him in spirit and in truth."

Worshipping God in spirit and in truth requires a family to understand the importance of corporate/family prayer in their household. The old adage "A family that prays together, stays together," cannot be stressed enough. Praying together will put the family into a worship mode. Worship brings you into the very presence of God. When your family is in the very presence of God, revelation knowledge comes forth. You are more cognizant of the attempts of the adversary to divide and conquer your house. Sit down with your family, men. Call a family meeting. Let them know what is happening and what God wants to be done to about the situation. When your family sees that you are leading them in every aspect of the word AND the WORD, they will respect and adhere to your directives.

Satan's desire is really to destroy the faith of one or more member's faith in God. Satan knows that obedience and faith go hand in hand in the life of a Christian. Who in the family would have the most trouble with two deep concepts like obedience and faith? Yes, your children. Satan will enter your home bringing a rebellious spirit to implant in your children. He will place them in opposition to their parents. If definitive behavior rules are not in place for the children, husband and wife may begin to lash at each other about the children's behavior because their parenting styles have not been shaped. Opposition, then, comes to the entire family. Everybody is coming home in the evening, going to their rooms, not talking to each other, sharing no quality time with each other - the family is in jeopardy. This is the time for Dad to rise up and take his position as spiritual head of the household. Bring the family together in prayer, praise, supplication, worship and thanksgiving and watch all the strongholds of the evil one come tumbling down. It is God's desire that the family unit remain strong in Him! Make it happen!

Families, beware when it looks like you have mastered your course. You begin to take pride in all that God is doing in your family. Your children are well-behaved, the marital relationship is firm - you are in control of the fate of your family. Satan again steps in, sits on your shoulder and whispers in your ear, Dad, "You no longer need God," or Mom, "The family doesn't need to pray as much. We are doing fine, now." Do not be deceived. A false sense of security is stepping in. The family begins to believe that they have achieved this wonderful state by themselves. Satan eases in and makes you or your wife a scoffer, which brings chaos into your family. You scoff at your friends, your neighbors, or even your church. Your children begin to brag at school at all the "things" they have acquired from their parents. The family is so full of pride now that they never realize what a scoffing attitude has invaded their household, because their focus has been shifted from a God-based family to a self-based family.

Your family has to be rooted and grounded in the Word of God - at all costs. Only through His Word does God give the family the information that they need to stand strong. In Psalms 34:7, God says that "The angel of the Lord encampeth round about them that fear him and delivered them." God not only gives the family His personal protection, but He also sends His angels to surround you with a hedge of protection from Satan. You are doubly blessed!

We can never stress enough that the leader of the household, the husband and father, has to love with the love of Jesus Christ. He is the family leader. Everything rises and falls with leadership. If the home is not going right, leadership needs to take a look within and at the total picture, go to the throne of grace and ask for guidance to put the home back in right relationship with God. Many of us are trying to run our homes by ourselves. Many of us, even Christians, are trying to run our homes without the church. The order God set up in the home is for the husband and father to be the leader of the home. The husband and father MUST adhere to God's plan for the family if the family is to be a glorious light for the world to see. The family that is doing all it can to do things God's way, glorifies God and lets the world know that it was designed for His glory and for His purpose.

The love of God for His Church composed of His families is the tie that binds Christians universally. God's Holy Spirit opens the door and leads you to the truth that is in Jesus Christ. That truth unveils a marvelous connection to the love he desires to inhabit your household - the love he describes in 1Corinthians:13. This is a demonstrative love, a love that leads the family to all the affection, attention, approval, acceptance and affirmation that they can desire.

CHAPTER 12

Love Never Fails

We have looked at the Biblical concepts of marriage and family in this book with the intention of teaching God's plan and desire for a unified Christian family. In the midst of all that we have presented, there is one concept that stands out above all that we have given - and that is love. John 3:16 states "For God so loved the world that He gave His only begotten Son that whosoever believeth in Him, should not perish but have everlasting life." This is the example of love to the highest degree - sacrificial love - a love that put everything else aside and brought forth salvation for all of us who believe. What a wonderful end result for such a horrific sacrifice!

Our families should be reflections of this powerful sacrificial love that 1Corinthians 13:8 says "....never faileth...." It is God's desire that Christians and their families portray that love not only to each other, but to the whole world. God's definition of love goes far beyond any emotion or feeling that man can ever conceive. It encompasses the depth and essence of His very being that allowed Him to understand our sinful nature and desire to do something to save us from eternal damnation.

The love expressed between husband and wife is a love that should most resemble the matchless love of God and for which He sacrificed His Son. The Son then demonstrated His love for that which He came to establish - the Church, by experiencing tremendous pain, suffering, and death. However, he showed us that we can achieve victory over Satan by His glorious resurrection on the third day.

Christ remained on earth 40 days to continue to prepare and train his disciples for the hard work ahead. He had to definitively set in action what He had already told them in His Great Commandment (Matthew 22:37-39): "Thou shalt love the Lord thy God with all thy heart, and with all thy soul, and with all thy mind. This is the first and great commandment. And the second is like unto it, Thou shalt love thy neighbor as thyself."

More often than not, Christians forget that the members of their households are also their neighbors. They show more love, attention, gratitude and appreciation for them than we do the members of our own households. Yes, we are to love others, but note we are to love others as we love ourselves. Those in the family are "ourselves". Love begins in the four walls of your home. Love begins with the head of the household, the husband and father, loving God with all of his might. He then shows his love to his wife in a way that matches the sacrificial love of Christ - a love that required Him to give His very life for His Church. Together, the couple, then brings their children into a circle of love called the family.

The family must form a circle. A circle is an unstoppable 360 degrees. There are no breaks in a circle - just an endless line that maintains itself in a circular motion. Even if something cuts a circle drawn on a piece of paper, the image of the circle still remains. You cannot pull a circle a loose. You cannot move a piece of a circle to another portion of the page. A circle drawn on a sheet of paper is truly endless.

This is God's plan for marriage and the family - that they form an unbroken circle. Nothing can come between it, nothing can break it, nothing can change the shape of it. No matter what happens, it still remains a circle. It is an infinite circle of love that passes from generation to generation. All Praise be to God!

Notes